THIS NOTEBOOK BELONGS TO

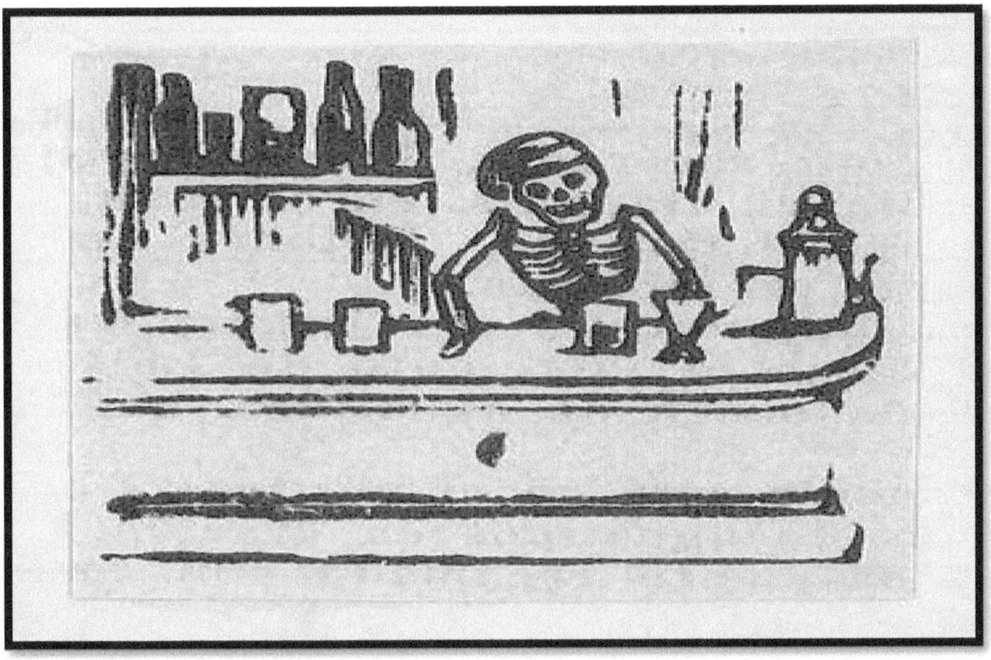

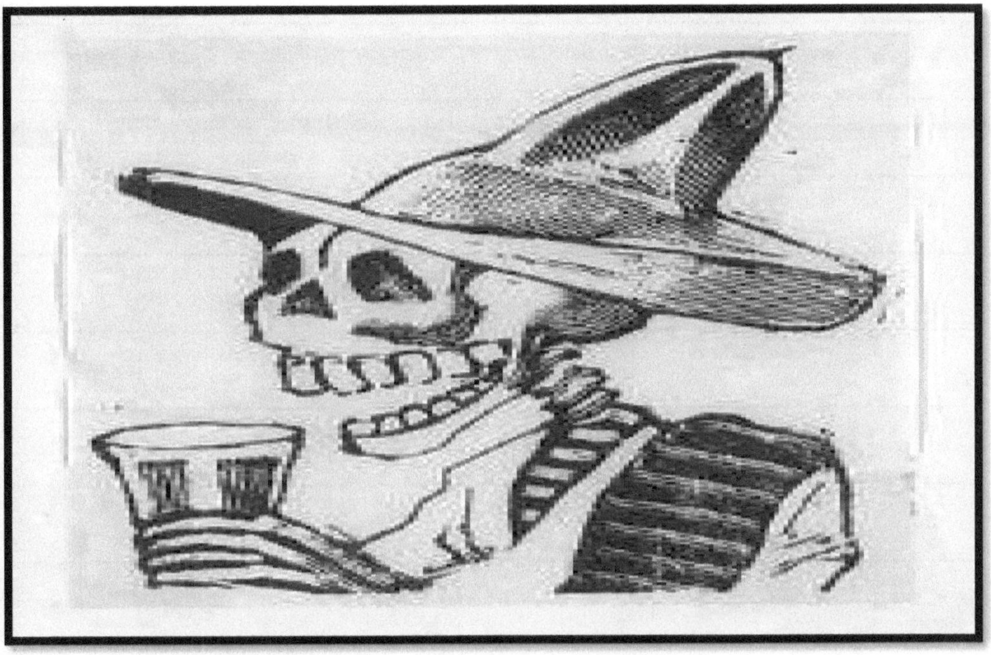

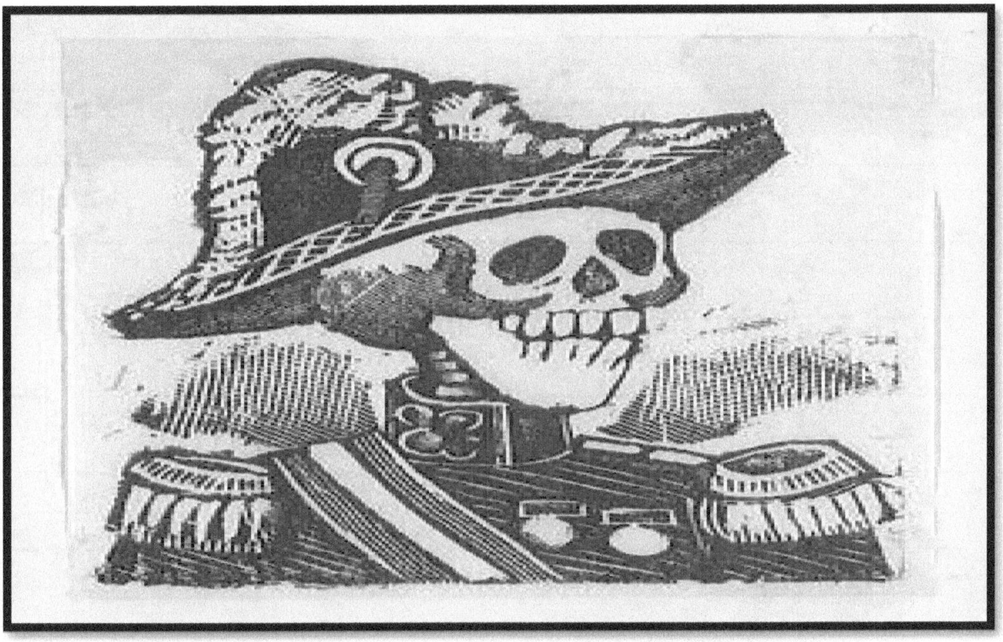

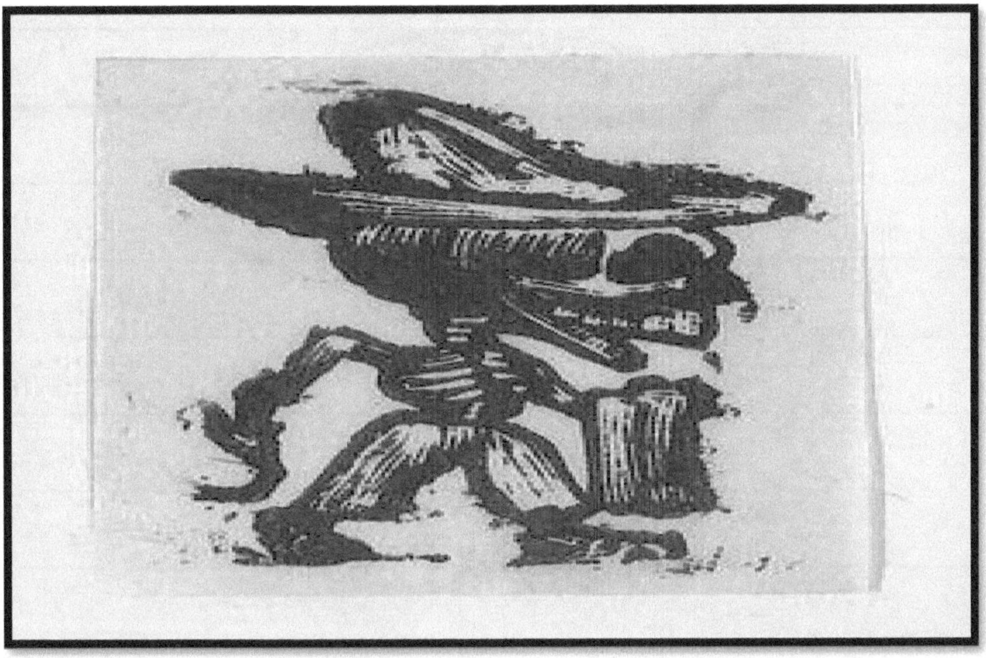

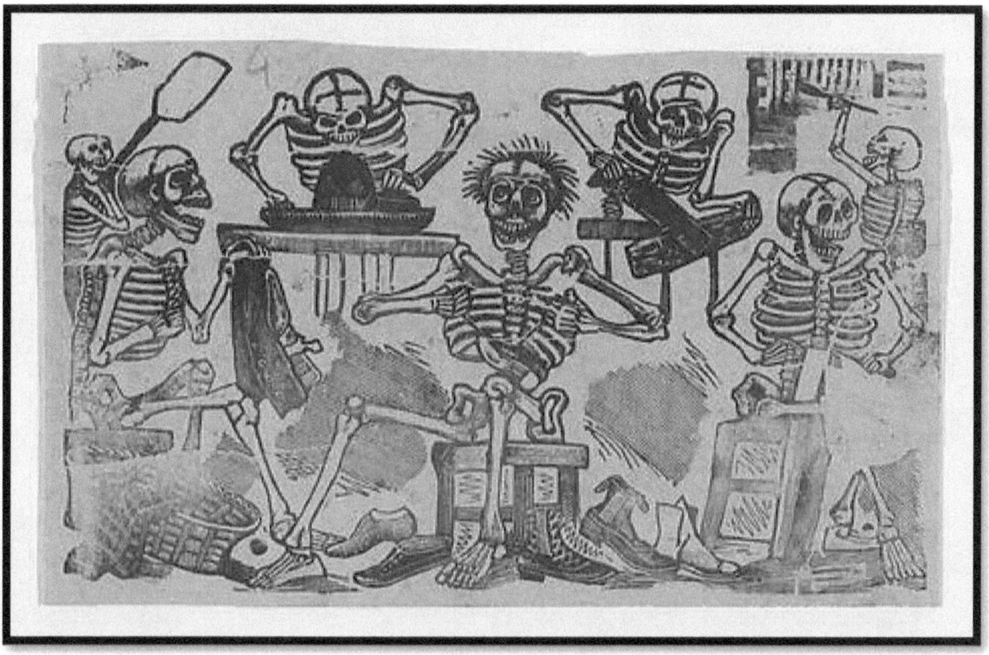

www.ingramcontent.com/pod-product-compliance
Lightning Source LLC
Chambersburg PA
CBHW030946240526
45463CB00016B/1976